Se

MW01133488

Funny & Weird

Marine Animals

By

P. T. Hersom

Hersom House Publishing

Ocala, Florida

Sea Life Funny & Weird Marine Animals

By P. T. Hersom

© Copyright 2013 P. T. Hersom

Reproduction or translation of any part of this work beyond that permitted by section 107 or 108 of the 1976 United States Copyright Act without permission of the copyright owner is unlawful. Requests for permission or further information should be addressed to the author.

This publication is designed to provide accurate and authoritative information in regard to the subject matter covered. It is sold with the understanding that the publisher is not engaged in rendering legal, accounting, or other professional services. If legal advice or other expert assistance is required, the services of a competent professional person should be sought.

First Published, 2013

Printed in the United States of America

Hersom House Publishing

3365 NE 45th St., Suite 101

Ocala, Florida 34479

This book is dedicated to my funny and weird seven year old grandson, Cameron. As unique as the marine animals are... so is he. With Cameron's humor and quirky antics, intertwined with pure intelligence, he inspires me in ways that only a grandson can do.

Love ya, Cameron!

Carpet Shark or Wobbegong

Size: Up to 10 feet in length.

Where they live: Tropical waters of the western Pacific Ocean and eastern Indian Ocean.

What they like to eat: Mollusks, fish and crustaceans.

Tell Me More

The carpet or wobbegong sharks get their name from the strange ornate patterns that cover their skin, giving them the appearance of a carpet. This built in camouflage is further enhanced by little weed like whiskers that surround their mouths and act as sensory barbs. They are a bottom dwelling shark and mainly are seen on the ocean floor resting. They do not pose a threat to humans unless they are provoked.

Christmas Tree Worm

Size: 2 to 6 inches in height.

Where they live: On coral in tropical oceans from the Caribbean to the Indian and Pacific.

What they like to eat: Microorganisms from the water.

Tell Me More

Christmas tree worms are brightly multicolored tube-building worms and live on coral reefs. They get their name from their two crowns or spirals that are shaped like Christmas trees. These spirals are actually mouth appendages that catch microorganisms and transport the food down the Christmas tree like branches into the worm's mouth. These same spirals structures are used for breathing and can also be called "gills".

Colossal Squid

Size: Up to 46 feet long and over 1,000 lbs.

Where they live: Southern ocean regions worldwide, in depths up to over 7,000 feet.

What they like to eat: Large fish, marine worms and other squid.

Tell Me More

Colossal squid are the largest of the squid family and tend to live in the southern ocean regions of the world. Colossal squid are thought to be the monster of many old sailor legends.

Different from any other squid, most only have suckers lined with small teeth, on their tentacles. The colossal squid has sharp hooks, some three pointed hooks, and even with the ability to swivel on their tentacles. Their bodies tend to be heavier and wider than the giant squid, while their tentacles shorter in length and their mantles longer in length. They also have the largest eyes in the animal kingdom, one eye known to measure 11 inches across!

Sperm whales and other whales are known to feed on colossal squid and their beaks have been found in whale stomachs. Whales that feed on the colossal squid tend to have scars around their mouth and head from encounters with the colossal squid's sharp hooks on their tentacles.

Longhorn Cowfish

Size: Up to 20 inches in length.

Where they live: Around reefs of the tropical and subtropical Indo-Pacific ocean regions.

What they like to eat: Algae, crustaceans, worms, sponges and small fish.

Tell Me More

Longhorn cowfish are part of the boxfish family and get their name from their long horns on top of their heads, which resemble a longhorn cow. They have a comical look, with very prominent lips that can appear as if they are puckering up for a big kiss.

Longhorn cowfish come in several colors ranging from yellow, orange and green with many having blue and/or white spots. Longhorn cowfish are poisonous to eat and have two natural built in defenses to ward off potential predators. First they have their horns, the two on top of their head and two more horns beneath their tail. This makes them difficult to swallow. And secondly, they release a poisonous toxin when startled by bright lights or loud sounds, or when threatened by a predator.

Cowfish are slow swimmers and may appear to be hovering in the water because of their unique way of using their dorsal and pectoral fins. This form of swimming is called ostraciform swimming. Because of their unique form of swimming cowfish are easily caught by divers and are known to make grunting sounds. This fish is seen on the cover of the book too.

Cuttlefish

Can you find the cuttlefish?

Size: Up to 20 inches in length.

Where they live: Tropical waters of the world except around North and South America.

What they like to eat: Crustaceans, worms, fish, octopuses and other cuttlefish.

Tell Me More

Cuttlefish belong to the same marine animal family as octopuses and squid, like their cousins they have the ability to shoot ink to evade predators and have poisonous spit, which they use to paralyze their prey once caught within their tentacles and bitten by their beak.

Now let's talk about what makes the cuttlefish different. Did you know that the cuttlefish can change their color in mere seconds at will? That's why they are also called the "chameleons of the sea" they can easily camouflage themselves to look like their surroundings. They avoid predators by using rocket propulsion, water is squeezed down within their body into a special tubular muscle, like a siphon, controlling the direction and quickly propelling them backwards.

Cuttlefish have a W-shaped eye, and amazingly can see both frontwards and backwards at the same time! They possess an internal structure called cuttlebone (the things you see in bird cages) it has small chambers and similar to a submarine, releasing or filling the chambers with gas control the cuttlefish's buoyancy.

Now for the really amazing facts, did you know that cuttlefish have three hearts and blue-green blood? Three separate hearts work like this, one for each gill and one for the rest of the body, and the reason their blood is blue-green, is because of the protein hemocyanin, which has copper in it rather than hemoglobin.

Dogface Pufferfish

Size: Up to 13 inches in length.

Where they live: Tropical waters of the Indian and Pacific Ocean.

What they like to eat: Sponges, stony coral, algae and crustaceans.

Tell Me More

Now this fish lives up to its name, with its big sad puppy eyes, looks just like a cute little doggie. Not only appropriately named for its appearance, but also its behavior, the dogface pufferfish is rarely aggressive and tends to live in solitary among the tropical reefs.

They usually have random dark spots on a colored body, ranging in colors from browns, grays, bluish yellows, black and gold or orange. When frightened or distressed by potential predators, pufferfish can inflate their bodies to over two times their original size by swallowing air or water. They also secrete a toxic poison, a natural defense against predators.

Elephant Fish or Elephant Shark

Size: Up to 5 feet in length.

Where they live: Subtropical waters of the southwest Pacific Ocean around Australia and New Zealand.

What they like to eat: Small fish, crustaceans and bottom living invertebrates.

Tell Me More

Elephant fish have a long "trunk like" snout that looks similar to an elephant's trunk. They are found in the deep-sea were they like to feed off the muddy and sandy bottom of the ocean, eating shellfish and small fish.

Since they spent most of their time in deep waters up to 4500 feet, when captured and brought to the surface their eyes are a startling metallic green color. The elephant shark is harmless to humans.

Flamingo Tongue Snail

Size: 1 to 2 inches long.

Where they live: On soft coral in the Western Atlantic Ocean throughout the Caribbean Sea, Lesser Antilles and the Gulf of Mexico.

What they like to eat: Soft coral.

Tell Me More

The Flamingo Tongue Snail is a small yet beautiful, brightly colored sea snail that lives among the coral. They many times are collected by snorkelers and scuba divers because of what appears to be their colorful shell. However, unknown to most, the snail's shell color is actually a solid orange or white color.

The black spotted colorful design of the snail is the soft mantel tissue that covers its shell.

Flying Fish

Size: Up to 16 inches in length.

Where they live: In all oceans worldwide.

What they like to eat: Plankton.

Tell Me More

Flying fish are so much fun to watch, one time while sailing in the Caribbean several of these fish flew right on to the deck of our catamaran. Flying fish do not actually fly, but glide through the air. This is their way of escaping from predators and this is how they do it.

Swimming fast through the water they leap into the air and expand their pectoral fins, which are long like wings, this allows them to glide through the air over the water for long distances. Flying fish have been recorded at speeds up to 43 mph, and flight durations up to 45 seconds long. In addition, flying fish have been recorded to glide a distance of 1300 feet.

Frogfish

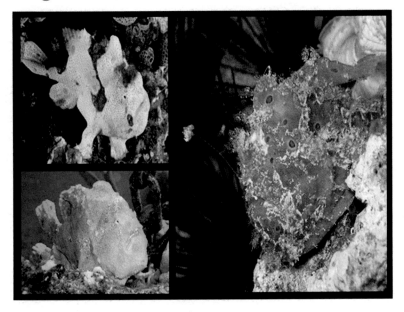

Size: 1 to 15 inches in length.

Where they live: In coral and rock reefs of most tropical and subtropical oceans and seas worldwide.

What they like to eat: Fish and crustaceans.

Tell Me More

Frogfish are the masters of disguise and can conceal themselves from both predators and prey.

Belonging to the anglerfish family they are equipped in front with a "rod" like dorsal fin that is topped with an esca, or "lure". It is like having their very own, fishing rod and lure. Though the "rod" dorsal fin does not change much in appearance between different types of frogfish, the "lure" may. It can mimic, that means to look like, a tubeworm, a shrimp or another fish, or simply just a lump of something.

As the frogfish hides himself among the coral and reef, it patiently waits for something to be attracted to its lure. Then when the prey gets close enough, it quickly snatches it into its mouth. The attack from the frogfish can be as quick as 6 milliseconds and they can swallow something up to twice their own size!

Frogfish can hide so well because they do not have scales like other fish and their bodies are covered with bumpy bifurcated spinules. Plus they have many colors like red, green, yellow, white and black, even spots to help them blend into the coral reef. Many frogfish can even change colors. Can you pick out all the frogfish in the photos?

Monkfish or Allmouth

Size: 4 to 5 feet in length.

Where they live: Northwest Atlantic Ocean.

What they like to eat: Fish.

Tell Me More

Monkfish are part of the anglerfish family and live on the bottom of the ocean. Like other anglerfish, monkfish hide on the ocean floor and then attract their prey with a lure. In their case it's called the "esca", which is a part of their spine which can be angled forward, so it can dangle over their mouth and wiggled like bait. Can you see the monkfish hiding in the picture?

Monkfish have very wide and flat heads that are as broad as the fish is long, with enormous mouths filled with long sharp teeth. That is why they are also called "allmouth" since the fish is mostly head, and almost the whole head is mouth. They have been known to eat prey nearly one-half their size, as well as eat water birds on the surface.

Monkfish are considered to be a very good tasting fish to eat. Their tail meat is known to taste like, and have the same texture of lobster tail meat, hence they've been nicknamed, "the poor man's lobster". The largest monkfish caught on record weighed 253 lbs. That had to be one big mouth!

Oarfish

Size: Up to 56 feet in length.

Where they live: Oceans worldwide.

What they like to eat: Jellyfish, crustaceans, squid and small fish.

Tell Me More

Seeing a living oarfish is a very rare occurrence since they spend most of their time in the deeper deaths of the ocean. When they have been seen near the surface it has been because they were dying or sick.

Oarfish are also known as "King of the Herrings" because they are part of the herring family and are the longest boney fish in the world.

Their "kingly" looking dorsal fin originates from above the eyes and runs the entire length of the oarfish; around 400 dorsal fin rays in all, the first 12 are elongated to varying lengths, forming a trailing crest with reddish spots and flaps of skin at the ends, giving the appearance of a kingly headdress.

Because of this silver tapering, ribbon like body, along with the impressive pinkish to cardinal red dorsal fin, give the oarfish the perception of majesty, and help explain how they became the center of many sea serpent tales.

Ocean Sunfish

Size: Up to 10 feet in length and 2200 lbs.

Where they live: Tropical waters of all oceans.

What they like to eat: Jellyfish, squid, eel grass, small fish and crustaceans.

Tell Me More

Sunfish look like a big fish head with a tail and can be just as tall as they are long. Sunfish are the heaviest bony fish in the world and received their name from being seen floating on the ocean surface sunbathing. Sunfish while basking in the surface sun, allow seabirds to feed on parasites that lodge within their skin.

They range in color from white, grey, silver and brown. Even though sunfish are very large they still have to watch out for predators that would like to have them for lunch, like the killer whale, sea lions and sharks.

They are known to be very friendly and docile around divers. Injuries from sunfish occur more to boats from accidently hitting the enormous fish basking on the surface. The largest sunfish caught on record is 3500 lbs. In comparison, a Toyota Camry weighs 3200 lbs.

Pinecone Fish or Pineapple Fish

Size: Up to 12 inches in length.

Where they live: The tropical and subtropical regions of the Indo-Pacific oceans.

What they like to eat: Plankton, shrimp and fish.

Tell Me More

Pinecone fish have a yellow to orange colored round body that has large scales, with very prominent ridges on them. These ridges are outlined in black, giving the fish the appearance of a pinecone or pineapple; hence their name seems to fit very well.

Pinecone fish are very popular among public aquariums worldwide, not only because of their unique pinecone look, but their glowing smile due to the bioluminescent bacteria that live in the sides of their mouths. The color of the bioluminescence produces a glow, blue-green to yellow, that attracts plankton on which they feed on at night.

The pinecone fish is considered nocturnal and prefers to hide during the day.

Red-lipped Batfish

Size: Up to 16 inches in length.

Where they live: Galapagos Islands.

What they like to eat: Small fish and crustaceans.

Tell Me More

At first glance you might think this little fish is ready to go on a date, since she has her red lipstick on. Well we don't know if she going on a date, but we definitely know why this little fish is appropriately named, the red-lipped batfish.

Batfish are actually not very good at swimming as most fish, so they use their pectoral fins to "walk like" on the bottom of the ocean. Batfish have a boney crown on top of their head called a illicium, which they use as a lure to attract their next meal.

Sarcastic Fringehead

Size: Up to 12 inches in length.

Where they live: Pacific Ocean off the coast of North America.

What they like to eat: Crustaceans.

Tell Me More

This fish looks like it's the star in a monster movie!

Sarcastic fringehead are ferociously territorial and very aggressive. When there is a turf war between two sarcastic fringeheads, the mouth wrestling begins! They begin wrestling with their large mouths fully extended against one another as if they were kissing, until one of them gains dominance.

You'll find fringehead fish setting up house in empty clam or snail shells, abandoned burrows, and cracks in rock outcroppings. Primarily ambush predators, they like to hide within their shelter and then surprise prey swimming or moving by their hideout.

Sea Pig

Size: 6 inches in length.

Where they live: Deep on the bottoms of the Indian, Atlantic and Pacific Oceans.

What they like to eat: Deep-sea mud.

Tell Me More

Sea pigs live on the bottom of the ocean and are part of the sea cucumber family. Like nature's very own vacuum cleaner, they eat the sediments of the deep-sea mud which is loaded with rich organic particles. This rich organic food has sifted down from the surface of the ocean and come to rest on the bottom of the sea, creating food for the sea pigs, such as, dead plants and fish.

Sea pigs have large tube feet, two of their feet even look like antennas on top of their head. Sea pigs also have tentacles which they use to find food and to feed themselves. As they feed on the deep-sea mud they are introducing oxygen into the sediment and making it now habitable by other myriad small creatures.

Shovelnose Guitarfish or Shovelnose Ray

Size: 4 ½ feet in length.

Where they live: Coastal waters of central California to the Sea of Cortez.

What they like to eat: Small fish, crustaceans, worms and mollusks.

Tell Me More

Shovelnose guitarfish are very unique in that they have characteristics of both sharks and rays, even though they are considered to be part of the ray family of marine animals. Their long pointed shovel like snout and triangular shaped head, give the shovelhead its well deserved name.

Shovelheads may live up 16 years and are considered harmless to humans because of their tooth structure. If one were to bite you, the worst that could happen is that you would get a good "gumming". I think he's smiling at you!

Stargazer

Size: Up to 3 feet in length.

Where they live: Tropical waters of most southern ocean regions of the world.

What they like to eat: Fish and crustaceans.

Tell Me More

Stargazers are unique in that they have their eyes, nostrils (nose) and mouth located on top of their head. They burrow themselves into the sand on the bottom of the ocean floor until only their eyes can be seen. Then wait for some prey to walk or swim by, then surprise attack their unsuspecting prey.

Stargazers do not have scales and are silver or pale in color, some with spots covering their bodies. They are equipped with a cirri on the edge of their mouth that helps prevent sand from coming in when their hiding and waiting for prey.

Stargazers not only look scary, but can deliver some scary pain to other predators with their poisonous spines located above the pectoral fin and behind the opercle fin. Plus they have the ability to deliver up to 50 volts of electric shock through their modified eye muscles!

Napoleon Wrasse or Maori Wrasse

Size: Males can reach 6 feet, and females up to 3 feet long. And grow to over 400 lbs.

Where they live: Around coral in the Indo-Pacific Ocean regions.

What they like to eat: Fish, shellfish, starfish, sea urchins, mussels and worms.

Tell Me More

The napoleon wrasse is one of the biggest coral reef fishes in the world and can easily be recognized by its shape, size and beautiful color. The male wrasse, are a bright blue and green, to a purplish blue color, while the females generally range in a red-orange and white color. They have a hump over their head that grows with age and looks like a napoleon hat, hence their name.

Wrasses are equipped with protrusible mouths, which separate their jaw teeth and jut outward. This allows them to smash big chunks of dead coral with peg-like teeth to feed on the mussels and worms inside. They play a vital role in balancing the coral reef marine life by being one of the few predators of poisonous marine animals like the boxfish, sea hares and crown-of-thorns starfish.

The wrasse though large, are gentle giants, and on many occasions have been known to interact playfully with divers much like a pet dog would do, by brushing or nudging up against a diver to get attention, like a dog wanting to be petted.

Wrasse can live up to 30 years and are known to be "protogynous hermaphrodites" which means some of the female wrasse become male at around 9 years of age. The reason why or how this happens is still known.

Yeti Crab or Kiwa

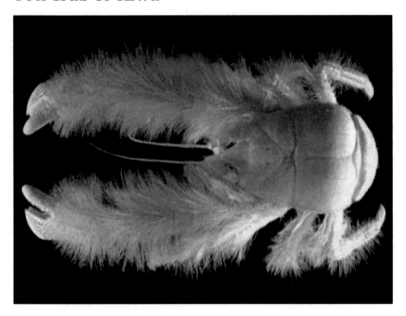

Size: 6 inches long.

Where they live: South Pacific Ocean and Antarctica, near volcanic and hydrothermal vents.

What they like to eat: Bacteria and scavenging.

Tell Me More

The white ghostly looking yeti crab or kiwa, was discovered recently in the depths of waters of Antarctica near volcanic hydrothermal vents. The name "yeti crab" describes the silky white, furry like hair, called setae, that covers their claws and legs.

Like many creatures that live at extreme depths, in this case 7500 to 8500 feet, the yeti crab is considered to be blind because of the lack of pigment in their eyes. However, that does not stop them from being good hunters of food. They are generally thought to eat the bacteria that feed on the minerals coming out of the volcanic hydrothermal vents.

Funny Creatures to Tickle Your Funny Bone

What Did You Learn Today? Questions

1. Do carpet sharks like to eat people?
2. Christmas tree worms grow as big as Christmas trees, true or false?
3. What fish is also called, "The King of the Herrings"?
4. Do stargazer fish have scales?
5. Which fish is known for mouth wrestling?
6. Which fish looks like man's best friend?
7. Why is it, that cuttlefish are called "chameleons of the sea"?
8. What fish is the heaviest bony fish in the world?
9. What fish is called, "the poor man's lobster" because it tastes so good?
10. The elephant fish has a long trunk like snout, like an elephant, true or false?
11. Red-lipped batfish can fly and only come out at night, true or false?
12. This fish's name sounds like it's the lead player in a rock band.
13. What does the sea pig like to eat?
14. The longhorn cowfish has a tail that looks like a cow's tail, true or false?
15. How fast can a flying fish fly?
16. The pinecone fish is also called by what name?
17. Frogfish like to eat insects, true or false?

18. What is the biggest squid in the world?

19. What fish likes to eat poisonous marine animals?

20. What crab lives around volcanic vents?

21. The flamingo snail has bright colored spots on its shell, true or false?

What Did You Learn Today? Answers

1) No, they like to eat fish, mollusks and crustaceans.

2) False, they grow up to 6 inches high.

3) The oarfish.

4) No.

5) The sarcastic fringehead.

6) The dogface pufferfish.

7) Because they can change their color in mere seconds at will.

8) The ocean sunfish.

9) The monkfish.

10) True.

11) False.

12) The shovelnose guitarfish.

13) Deep-sea mud.

14) False, they have horns that look like a cow's horns.

15) Up to 43 mph.

16) The pineapple fish.

17) False, they eat fish and crustaceans.

18) The colossal squid.

19) The napoleon wrasse.

20) The yeti crab.

21) False, the shell color is actually a solid orange or white color.

Enjoyed the Book?

Thank you for buying this book. I hope that you and your children enjoy reading the book and learning about the animals in the book as much as I did writing it. If you found the book enjoyable, please help me out by posting a review on the Amazon page. Thank you for taking the time to do so. It is very much appreciated.

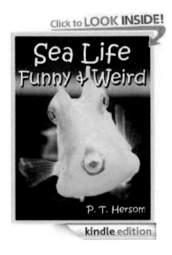

Other Books to Enjoy by P. T. Hersom

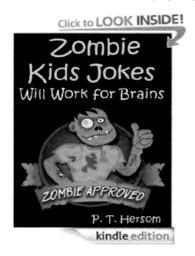

Zombie Party Ideas for Kids: How to Party Like a Zombie & Zombie Jokes: Will Work for Brains available in the Amazon Kindle and paperback.

Made in the USA
Middletown, DE
12 December 2019

80538260R00031